Spiritual Affirmations

Igniting Faith, Hope, Love, and Inspiration

STEPHANIE BAILEY
Miss-Adventures

Spiritual Affirmations

Igniting Faith, Hope, Love, and Inspiration

Spiritual Affirmations: Igniting Faith, Hope, Love, and Inspiration

Stephanie Bailey/Miss-Adventures

Copyright © 2024 Stephanie Bailey

Published by Miss-Adventures Publishing

Paperback ISBN: 979-8-9874383-3-6

For my stepsons, Bruno and Rocco Miller, so they unfailingly have a reminder that God is always with them—protecting, guiding, and assuring them with HIS unconditional love.

DEDICATION

I dedicate this book to everyone seeking a stronger faith, more profound spiritual life, positivity, and benevolent reminders that GOD loves you unconditionally.

I dedicate this book to my sister Tanya Garner whose God-fearing devotion inspires me, and to my sister Tasha Nix whose love for God keeps her strong.

I dedicate this book to God for showing and guiding me on this loving vision to bring more hope and faith to the world.

DISCLAIMER

I am so glad you are reading *Spiritual Affirmations: Igniting Faith, Hope, Love, and Inspiration.* Please realize that only you can transform the direction of your life by doing the necessary work. This book offers you another way to change your mindset and spiritual beliefs. These affirmations are not religious. Your problems will not disappear and your life will not be blissful and in perfect alignment if you drop to your knees, clasp your hands firmly, and say the Hail Mary nine times in front of a priest or nun. No offense to religions, but that is not my unrealistic goal for any reader. These affirmations I lovingly wrote are to open your mind, body, and soul to how a strong faith in God can change your life—creating new opportunities, choices, and steps for you to manifest the life the Divine created for you. I make no promises (or offer no guarantees) that the affirmations in this book will alter your life. Dark forces (Satan) will tempt you in order to challenge your belief that God is working for you. However, your beliefs are just that—yours. Spiritual Affirmations help guide you toward the life you envision for yourself—filled with faith, hope, love, and inspiration.

This book is not a substitute for actual therapy, a psychiatrist, a psychologist, or any licensed doctor's advice.

"Give your burdens to the Lord. And he will take care of you. He will not permit the godly to slip and fall."

—**Psalm 55:22**

"There is a difference between a trial and a temptation. The goal of a temptation is to see you fail. The goal of a trial is to see you succeed and get stronger. God won't tempt you but HE will test you by trials."

—Lead Pastor Jim Burgen
Flatirons Community Church

JOURNEY TO SPIRITUAL FAITH

*"God is faithful; he will not let you be tempted
beyond what you can bear. But when you are
tempted, he will also provide a way out so that
you can stand up under it."*

—1 Corinthians 10:13

As the phone slipped from my hands, dropping to the floor, I could feel my body separating as if I was floating away. I closed my eyes, and for a moment, I swear I could hear a pin drop. As my inhalations and exhalations sped up, the sound of my heartbeat filled my ears. I had to escape; out of this room, out of this building. I was suffocating in confusion and disbelief.

My legs started moving automatically shifting into a sprint. Get out, and get out quick. I felt like I was running on air down the hall and multiple levels of the Boston brownstone I lived in. Grasping for the massive door with the strength of *She-Hulk*—nothing would stop me from this urgent feeling to leave.

As I ran down Commonwealth Avenue, everything was a complete blur. My mind and body felt like I was on the *Bullet* train—moving as quickly as possible to reach my destination—except my route had no endpoint. This feeling was similar to when I ran the 50- and 100-yard races in high school. Except this wasn't a race I wanted to win. Instead, this felt like a race to survive—convincing myself that the faster I ran, the quicker I could turn back time and make everything right again.

Tears drenched my face. I did not know where I was going. I only knew I didn't want to stop. My breath started catching up to me, forcing me to slow down. I didn't want to stop. I couldn't stop. I had to keep going. But where?

"Stephanie, I'm so sorry to have to tell you…" kept running through my mind like a horrible nightmare I couldn't wake from no matter how hard I tried.

"Stephanie. Stephanie. STEPHANIE!" The ringing in my ears magnified until it pinpointed my friend Mariela's voice from a distance.

"Stephanie, please stop." Hearing her voice blocked my terror, hypnotizing my mind as my legs, feet, and

arms gradually slowed down. Eventually, gravity took over as my knees buckled to the pavement, forcing me to the ground in anguish.

Hyperventilating, I could feel Mariela's arms wrapping around me as I melted in hysteric disarray. As her hands scooped to lift me, I realized she had chased me down Commonwealth Avenue to the park, which I could barely recognize through my swollen eyes. *"I'm so sorry, Stephanie,"* came from Mariela's mouth. Her sympathetic words confirmed what I refused to hear—this dreaded nightmare I was in; I wasn't waking up any time soon.

> *"Be sober, be vigilant; because your adversary the devil, as a roaring lion, walketh about, seeking whom he may devour." —Peter 5:8*

There are moments in our lives when our faith is challenged. During these trials, we choose to either win or lose this battle to Satan. Because I felt emotionally defeated by my fathers death, I let Satan lead my life through temptations.

After my dad died, my life became a crazy, unpredictable roller-coaster ride, and those devastating words "I am so sorry, Stephanie," tormented my mind, body, and soul with so much anger toward God.

My dad dying of an unexpected heart attack at the age of fifty-three made no sense. Although he had high blood pressure he was healthy and worked out regularly. As a Presbyterian Minister and senior administrator of the *Synod of the Northeast*, my dad was a godly man who spent most of his life helping others, raising money to build free youth centers around the United States—providing hope and support to underprivileged kids. He created programs, communities, and funding for churches in need. My dad was my confidant, best friend, and a man I admired and looked up to for advice. God took my dad away, leaving my life filled with extreme highs and lows, trying to find ways to mend my broken, gutted heart on my own. No surprise, my already shaky faith in God crumbled.

> *My dad's death wasn't the first time Satan tried to defeat my soul and kill my spirit. However, losing my dad felt like Satan had finally won.*

Satan's first attack on my spirit started the day I was conceived through rape. The second was being molested multiple times before the age of three by men in the various foster homes I was in. The third attack was to chip away at my self-worth, as a wild child who was hard to understand—considered "difficult to raise"—which only caused me to act out even more like a *Tasmanian Devil*. The fourth attack, carrying around the heaviness of why my birth mother did not want me. The fifth, sixth, and seventh attacks, were my experiences of racism throughout the majority of my life, thoughts of suicide, and struggling to see my beauty and talents. Honestly, being sexually assaulted in college and my dad dying when I was only twenty years old felt like someone was throwing a deflated life jacket—when I was already barely staying above water. My spirit was exhausted, and Satan knew this.

> *Trying to present myself as "normal and OK" after my dad died was challenging.*

Growing up, my mom and I had an estranged relationship. Other than my siblings—who at the time I wasn't close to—I didn't know anyone my age who had a father who died. I felt utterly alone. Spiritually, mentally, and emotionally, I was astray. So, I did what many college students did: I drank like a frat boy and eventually turned to drugs.

I stopped drinking alcohol in 1992 but started smoking marijuana. I convinced myself that pot was healthier—even though I had a joint or blunt in my mouth the second my classes ended.

Growing bored with pot, I stopped smoking before graduating college. Moving to Denver in 1995, coping with the change of a new state, moving in with my mother, a new job, and new friends was tough mentally and emotionally.

In 1996, the drug ecstasy came into my life. At first, inducing a fourth of a pill seemed harmless. Feeling happy, smiling without having to try, and my sadness and pain melting away was a feeling I wanted to last forever. But nothing lasts forever. Being a control freak and still desiring not to deal with reality, cocaine became my next drug of choice.

Drugs were my way of numbing my pain. I didn't feel I had anyone or anything else to lean on without being judged emotionally. This feeling was the catalyst for attracting many men, relationships, and friendships that reflected how I felt about myself—unworthy of genuine love and success—so that I could continue to be a victim and my own enabler on this treacherous path I called my life.

I pushed away family and created distance with genuine friends because I did not want help. It's easy to tell yourself you are F.I.N.E (fucked up, insecure, neurotic, and emotional) when you surround yourself with individuals who mirror these similar traits. I enjoyed feeling numb and the victim of my circumstance.

For me, disowning God meant I would not say HIS name. Instead, I would say, "The Universe" and proclaim, "There is something greater out there guiding me." Through my lack of faith in God, I subconsciously gave Satan more power and control. Does this sound familiar?

The anger I felt in my heart toward God for my dad's abrupt heart attack was like *Hurricane Katrina* in Louisiana—out to destroy anything and everything that came too close to me, including myself. Without my dad, I was an abandoned ship lost at sea—drowning in my eternal sorrows. I needed my dad to be the captain of my boat, guiding me through these treacherous storms in my life.

Drugs made it easier for me to pretend to be F.I.N.E, and being happy was as easy as barricading my heart with deadbolts, daggers, and fire—anything to prevent me from getting hurt again. Protecting my heart was all too easy and familiar, however, usually not successful.

For most of us, there is a rock bottom moment we eventually hit, waking us. Hitting rock bottom will either remind us that we deserve better, or we will continue pulling ourselves deeper down the rabbit hole.

> *"The Lord is near to the brokenhearted and saves the crushed in spirit."* —Psalm 34:18

One night, as I looked in the bathroom mirror at a reflection I no longer recognized—rundown, sunken eyes and barely standing, unable to comprehend what day it was—I gazed down at the white-powered line I was about to snort at 3 am. As my hands shook, I put down the rolled up twenty dollar bill, dropped to my knees, and asked out loud, as tears streamed down my face, *"God, if you are real, I need a sign."* I repeated this prayer over and over again until I went to bed and fell asleep.

When I woke, I had an overwhelming sense this was not how my life was supposed to be. I pulled my weary body out of the bed I was sharing with my drug-dealing, cheating boyfriend (my rock bottom, and it wasn't pretty), rubbed my puffy eyes, gathered my belongings, and headed home—never looking back. God's signs only strengthened the louder I asked, the harder I prayed, and the more I affirmed HE was real.

Surrendering to my faith, praying, and affirming what I knew in my heart led me back to God and, eventually, Christ. My experiences are why I created *Spiritual Affirmations: Igniting Faith, Hope, Love, and Inspiration* so you know you can overcome anything as long as you believe.

Doubts, fears, insecurities, despair, brokenness, anger, self-loathing, hurt, and uncertainty will creep into your life when Satan is hard at work. However, you have a choice. You can believe you are deserving of all the bad things that come, or you can view these experiences as learning lessons that will make you stronger and wiser.

> *Hitting rock bottom, reignited my faith again, and by working on my self-love, I could let go of all the anger I felt.*

Satan only strikes when we are at our weakest moment. Losing my dad, relinquishing my faith in God, and entertaining toxic relationships and experiences solidified how vulnerable I had become. Working on myself and regaining my faith was challenging. Bumps and bruises have tested my faith. But I continued to pick myself up with my firm belief in God. I find gratitude in the simple things and forgiveness for people and situations I thought impossible. My strength, wisdom, and self-love only continued to expand.

With God, I stopped pushing away the meaningful friendships in my life and magnetized other incredible friendships. I reunited with my biological parents and siblings and I was baptized by choice as an adult—twice. I now have a loving, supportive relationship with my mother who raised me—something I wished for but didn't think possible growing up. I have reconnected and deepened my relationship with my sister D'Vorah, who is my biggest cheerleader, advisor, and best friend. And I have been blessed with a loving partner and his two sons. God is good!

Spiritual Affirmations: Igniting Faith, Hope, Love, and Inspiration is written to help you find a glimmer of light when you see only darkness. This book is to give you the spiritual ammunition you need in your battle with Satan and strengthen your mind with hope and positivity, and to remind you that God always has your back. The more you believe, the more you will see positive shifts in your life.

I hope my spiritual affirmations connect with your heart, help soothe your soul, illuminate your spiritual faith, and remind you that you can get through anything as long as you believe in God.

XOXO,

Stephanie, aka Miss-Adventures

BEST PRACTICES FOR UTILIZING SPIRITUAL AFFIRMATIONS

Hold *Spiritual Affirmations: Igniting Faith, Hope, Love, and Inspiration* in your hands. Place this book in whichever hand feels most comfortable, laying the opposite hand on top. Or place the book close by. Breathe deeply three times—slow inhales and even slower exhales. (If you have a heart condition, please talk with your doctor first regarding the best breathing practices for you.) Once you feel relaxed, ask out loud (if you are in a comfortable place to do so) nine times, *"God, what do I need to know right now?"* Keep your eyes closed (again, if this is comfortable for you), open this book to whatever page your hands guide you (there are no wrong way), open your eyes, and read the affirmation you are receiving.

Why is it essential to ask nine times, "What do I need to know?"

Nine is the most powerful number in numerology. If you multiply any number by nine, that product, in turn, adds up to nine (for example, 9 x 28 = 252 (2 + 5 + 2 = 9). Nine is the only number that comes back to itself. Expanding nine's positive energy around the question "God, what do I need to know right now?" will help to ignite the affirmation you need when using this book. *Spiritual Affirmations: Igniting Faith, Hope, Love, and Inspiration* has 135 (1 + 3 + 5 = 9) declarations inside this book. How wonderfully exciting and powerful! Just the right tools and practices at your fingertips.

"Now faith is the substance of things I hoped for, the evidence of things not seen."

—Hebrews 11:1

Spiritual Affirmations

*God never gives
me anything I can
not handle because
HE knows my
strength.*

*I will let go of
unnecessary
worry and stress
and instead give
it to God.*

God is protecting and guiding me.

*God guides me
in miraculous
ways.*

God knows everything, and HE is by my side. Today, I feel this the most.

I tap into the strength of my faith during this challenging moment.

*I am grateful
for all that God
provides.*

Forgiving others expands my heart and strengthens my faith.

Believing in what I cannot see and knowing all is possible brings me hope.

The answers I
need will appear
when I breathe,
let go, and trust
in God.

The most
important thing
is that God
loves me for
who I am.

Love is in my heart, faith is in my mind, and God is in my soul.

*I am a child of
God created in
HIS image of
love—and that's
all that matters.*

*Faith, love,
and hope will
conquer doubts
in my life.*

*Even if I cannot
see the path, God
is making a way.*

Blessings
continue to
unfold in my life.

I give praise in HIS name, and I feel incredible.

God opens my eyes and gives me the clarity to see the truth.

I will get through
this challenge with
the strength of
God by my side.

*I trust in the Lord
that everything
will be alright.*

Today, I embrace someone with kindness who needs it.

*My past mistakes,
failures, or
traumas do not
define my life.*

*I protect myself
with God's light
and love.*

*God, grant me
the strength to
get through today,
tomorrow, and
all the days ahead
with love and
perseverance.*

*I practice
forgiveness to
let more love in
my life.*

God, please give me the energy and will to get through this day with the power of YOUR love.

*I will let God
lead with
absolute trust in
the outcome.*

*God is bringing
love into my life.*

Today is full of blessings and goodwill.

With God on my side I will not fail.

God is guiding me through this storm and giving me the strength to keep pushing through.

I am learning and
growing from the
lesson(s) and tests
God sends me.

Thank you, God,
for believing in
me.

God is bringing
me what I need
and releasing
what I don't.

Thank you, God, for all that I've been through, for all that I have, and for all that continues to manifest in my life.

I lead my life in the loving direction God intended.

God's love for
me helps to heal
my past hurt
and pain.

*I let my faith
guide me with
confidence.*

When I feel tempted, I lean into God.

Gratitude and
grace abundantly
fill me.

I acknowledge the many blessings in my life.

God knows my actual plan on this Earth, and I trust HIM.

*Nothing is more
important than
my unwavering
faith and trust
in the Lord.*

*God is healing
my body in
miraculous ways.*

*Life is fantastic
when I let God
lead.*

*I look at others
and see God's
love.*

Thank you, God,
for all the
love that
surrounds me.

Grace, hope,
love, and
forgiveness
empower
my soul.

God knows
my heart and
soul, and HIS
knowing is all
that matters.

*My ambitions
and dreams come
to fruition when
I trust in God.*

God did not
create me to
be perfect; HE
created me to be
loving and kind.

God created me
to make mistakes
so I can learn and
grow stronger and
wiser emotionally
and mentally.

God created
me as HIS
loving child; my
parents were
only the vessel.

Forgiveness, compassion, and love are my number-one strengths.

I am worthy because God has unconditional love for me.

Today, I look around and fully take in the beauty God has created.

*God's love for
me inspires me.*

I am never alone; God is by my side.

My business is
flourishing in
God's grace.

*Love is in my
life, and it starts
with God first.*

*I feel utterly
blessed today.*

*I will heal,
overcome this
challenge, and find
gratitude through
God.*

God guides me
where I cannot
see and supports
me when I need
it the most.

*I breathe deeply
into my faith.*

Unconditional love
first starts with
God, then myself.

*God gives me
the clarity
I need.*

God's love is surrounding me, always.

*I faithfully know
everything will
be OK.*

My soul vibrates
when I say
God's praises.

*I am on the
direction God
has planned, not
the course I am
trying to lead.*

*I am praying for
those in need.*

*God will not
fail me.*

Satan has no power over my life.

I am grounded
and surrounded
by God's love.

I surrender to my faith to become more grounded, and my thoughts more clear.

*God guides me
in the direction I
need to go. I will
follow.*

I walk in my faith by treating others with kindness and respect.

*God does not
expect my life
to be perfect. I
release control.*

Everything
I need is in
my life.

*I release
judgment because
it's not my place
to judge others.*

*God fills my
heart with joy.*

*I am here for
a purpose and
ready to receive
God's plan.*

Every day I wake up is a blessing.

Thank you, God,
for showing me
that I am moving
in the right
direction.

God chose the parent(s) I have for my life.

I put my faith in the Lord; he will not fail me.

*Challenging
moments occur
to test my faith.*

*God, I need
you now, and
I can feel your
presence.*

*Thank you,
God, for my
health, wealth,
abundance, and
prosperity.*

Every time
I pray, I know
God is hearing me.

The Lord is my salvation, and God is my first love and life source.

*God enlightens
me to be the best
version of myself.*

*I am OK—God
is protecting me.*

God sees me for more than who I am.

I let go to let God in so I can release temptations.

*God is lifting me
and giving me
strength.*

I can get through anything with God by my side.

*I let go of the
people holding
me down so God
can provide me
with those who
uplift me.*

When I close my
eyes, I feel the
magnitude of
God's love.

*I feel God's
mighty forces
working on my
behalf.*

Nothing can hold me back from God's grace.

Serenity and peace surround me with loving white light.

I let go of this internal battle and release it to God.

*God is giving
me the time I
need to heal and
rejuvenate.*

*I praise God for
the life I have.*

The Lord loves me
and saves me.

*I give my
burdens to God
so that I can
take care of
myself.*

*God compels
my heart to
give without
expecting to
receive.*

*I know that God
is working for
my greater good.*

Possible things
are happening in
impossible moments
through God.

I will not be
defeated. I will live
my best self—God
is pulling me up.

*God reveals the
truth I seek in
HIS time.*

My battles are
not my battles
alone with God
in my life.

*I surrender
and give my
challenges to
God.*

God brings me
strength and
hope when I feel
there is none.

*I hold onto my
faith in moments
of despair.
God will get me
through this.*

*God is guiding
me through all
obstacles.*

*All will be OK
because God has
a greater plan
for me.*

*God is
mending the
relationships that
are essential to
my life.*

*My trust in the
Lord will reveal
the answers I need.*

Thank you,
God, for my
family, friends,
and those who
support me.

*Through the
Lord, my body
is healing.*

God will heal
the pain in my
heart in time.

I forgive in God's name to let go of anger and pain that do not serve my life.

*I trust the path
God is leading
me on.*

With God
by my side,
life is happening
for me, not
against me.

I know in my
mind, body, and
soul that God is
with me.

*God is my first
priority.*

I repent of my wrongdoings so they no longer control my life.

The Lord
forgives me and
surrounds me
with love.

God provides the
answers I need.

*God strengthens my
body, and Christ
heals my soul.*

There is nothing greater or more relevant than my love for the Lord.

God loves me for who I am.

Possibilities are
endless with
God.

CONCLUSION

"FAITH TELLS ME THAT NO MATTER WHAT LIES AHEAD OF ME, GOD IS ALREADY THERE."

—Anonymous

After utilizing *Spiritual Affirmations: Igniting Faith, Hope, Love, and Inspiration*—I hope your mind, body, and soul feel uplifted and more connected to God, knowing HE is serving your greater good.

Connecting with your spirituality doesn't mean you will never face obstacles, challenges, and trauma, which might try to irreparably break you. Faith implies that you have something other than yourself to lean on, guide you, and protect you. An unwavering belief in God gives you the power to get through the darkest moments when you can't see the light at the end of the tunnel. I have witnessed this miraculous shift in my life multiple times and in the lives of other people I know.

Conviction in God gives us hope, inspiration, and more profound inner strength instead of being dependent on alcohol, drugs, sex, hurting ourselves, and behaving recklessly to "get you through" the stresses and difficult moments life brings. Keeping it real, temptations are easy to fall into. However, it is your enduring faith that will pull you out and make you stronger.

You are never walking through this world alone. Giving God praise, prayers, and glorifying moments is easy when life is great. The real challenge is having hope in your darkest moments when you cannot see the outcome. When you can believe without a doubt, your life will turn around in positive and uplifting ways. Prayers, affirmations, and mantras help give you strength and guidance for the challenges you experience.

Focusing on the negative will only bring more of what you don't want into your life—destroying your conviction. This same magnetic energy will favorably flow when you stay strong in your faith. God works in divine ways when you unconditionally love and believe in HIM.

Continue to use *Spiritual Affirmations: Igniting Faith, Hope, Love, and Inspiration* to focus on the things that work in your life and empower you to not let temptations take over. I encourage you to develop your devotional prayers and affirmations, which continue to ignite your beliefs and strengthen your spiritual journey.

xoxo,

Stephanie

AFFIRMATIONS/PRAYERS YOU
FEEL INSPIRED TO WRITE

_____

_____

_____

_____

_____

_____

_____

_____

_____

_____

_____

_____

_____

_____

_____

_____

SPIRITUAL AFFIRMATIONS

_____

_____

_____

_____

_____

_____

_____

_____

_____

_____

_____

_____

_____

_____

_____

_____

_____

_____

BEYOND GRATEFUL

Thank you to everyone who has purchased *Spiritual Affirmations: Igniting Faith, Hope, Love, and Inspiration* and for your continued support, encouragement, and love.

Mom, I know in my heart and soul that God brought us together for you to be my mother. Thank you for adopting, raising, loving me, and teaching me many things I use today. You are a big part of who I am, and I am so grateful for you. Thank you Mary Roberts Bailey for being my mom and for all your love and support.

Thank you to my love, partner, and best friend, Damon Miller, for all the journeys we have explored together and for choosing me every day. Our journey has been challenging. However, it is our journey, and I'm glad we chose each other to explore life together. Your support and belief in me means the world. Love you, Bae!

SPIRITUAL AFFIRMATIONS

I have so much gratitude and love in my heart to my sister, D'Vorah Bailey, for helping me edit my book and for your love, support, and encouragement I felt when writing this second affirmations book—and all the other books I've written. You are the best sister in this world I could have grown up with even through our differences. All of your support and encouraging words during my health issues reminded me that I was never alone. I love you so much. My life wouldn't be the same without you as my biggest cheerleader!

I am utterly grateful to you, Kimberly Malone. Your thoughtfulness, support, creative advice, encouragement, unconditional love, and always being there when I need you goes beyond words. You inspire my life, and I can not imagine a world without you. Thank you for being my best friend, family, soul sister, and person. Thank you for helping to format my book cover, and creating my book's mock up for marketing, as well as providing me with the beautiful "second home" I need for girl time and writing. Love you, lady.

Thank you to my sister, best friend, person and confidant, Tanya Garner, for not only being a host with me on our podcast *Sisters On Love, Life, and Keeping It Real* but also loving me unconditionally. Thank you for believing in me, your listening ear, and for opening your life to me when God brought us together in 2007. Most importantly, thank you for being you—your strength and perseverance inspires my life.

Thank you, Gwieneverea Brandon, for being my best friend since we were five and for your unconditional love and prayers throughout my life—when I needed them the most. Thank you for hearing and listening to me when I was sick and getting my health back on track. You are the best Doctor! Love you so much!

Krista Zizzo, you have one of the kindest and most thoughtful souls I know. Thank you for being my friend, neighbor, cheerleader, and support team. The "mini copies" of my books you gift to me every time I write and publish a new book inspire and encourage me to continue to write. You are a blessing, my friend. Love you.

Thank you, Paulette Henson, for your friendship, unconditional love and support, which means the world to me. You are a powerhouse, my friend, and

I'm honored to be in your world. Cheers to all the success we keep creating together and separately. Love you, friend.

Thank you, Karen Robinson, for coming into my life and writing the thoughtful and touching review for the back of my book. I love your devotion to empowering women who have experienced trauma. You are an angel sent from heaven, my friend.

Loving thank you to all my family and close friends for being in my life. Every adventure I take is always more meaningful with you all in my life and by my side.

I am immensely grateful for *Flatirons Community Church*, Lead Pastor Jim Burgen, and (traveling) pastor Ben Foote. Through my trials and tribulations, your sermons and words, and *Flatirons Church* community—whether online or attending the Denver campus—have uplifted, inspired, and helped my life beyond words.

Thank you, Tiffany McBride, for illustrating the front and back covers for *Spiritual Affirmations: Igniting Faith, Hope, Love, and Inspiration*. Thank you for seeing my vision again and turning my vision into a beautiful reality. You are an extraordinarily gifted and talented artist, writer, and friend who I feel blessed to have in my life. Love you lady!

I have so much gratitude for Tara Backes, my web designer. Thank you for creating my marketing materials, keeping my website updated, and my launch team informed. You are a big part of my business; I'm so lucky to have you.

Maggie McLaughlin, I don't know what I would do without you. Thank you for formatting my book. I am immensely grateful for your knowledge and all that is needed to get books published successfully on Amazon, Goodreads, Barnes & Noble, Ingram Spark, etc. Thank you, thank you, thank you!

Thank you, Joseph Ferry, for editing my book; I am so grateful for your expertise and editing skills while keeping my voice as the writer.

Thank you to my publicist, Gail Snyder, for all your hard work getting my press release out; you are incredibly talented at what you do.

ABOUT THE AUTHOR

"My faith and love in God is not about perfecting my life, it's about strengthening my soul."

Do you want to feel happy and confident? Do you want to feel the love you deserve and the love you put into the world? Do you want to enhance and empower various aspects of your life? Welcome to Miss-Adventures Love Coaching.

Stephanie Bailey is the CEO of Miss-Adventures, LLC, has been a Love Mentor, Expert, and Coach for more than 26 years, Master Life Coach, three-time #1 Bestselling Author (*25 Tools For Goddesses, Miss-Adventures Guide To Ultimate Empowerment For Women: Harness Your Power and Thrive In Every Area of Your Life* and *99 Types Of Guys: A Humorous*

Collection of Dating Tips and Misadventures), and #1 New Release (*Love Affirmations: Manifesting the Life You Desire*). Stephanie has been a published writer, public speaker, podcaster, and Corepower Yoga Teacher for more than 15 years. Stephanie is spiritual and strongly believes in God and Christ and that powerful prayers and affirmations help ignite and create the love, health, wealth, success, family, abundance, relationships, and prosperity we want. Stephanie's mission is to help empower women on their journey and create a more straightforward path for guiding them to love. Self-love is the key. Stephanie offers in-person and virtual love coaching sessions.

To stay in touch with Stephanie, follow her on her social media platforms and visit her website, Miss-Adventures.com or scan the QR code below for Love Coaching advice, sessions, and packages.

Connect with Stephanie:

Website: https://www.miss-adventures.com

Email: missadventureslovecoach@yahoo.com

Instagram: @miss_adventures_coach

Facebook Page: @missadventuresseries

LinkedIn: linkedin.com/in/miss-adventures

Hubpages: miss-adventures.hubpages.com (relationship/love articles)

YouTube: Sisters On Love, Life and Keeping It Real

Thank you, God, for all the people in my life who have been supportive: my family, friends, and loving congregation at *Flatirons Community Church*. Thank you, God, for guiding me on my new affirmations book in your name and in the name of Christ—*Spiritual Affirmations: Igniting Faith, Hope, Love, and Inspiration*, and for helping me craft this beautifully divine book. My heart is immensely grateful to be able to spread spirituality, love, joy, hope, connection, and faith throughout the world. God, with you, all things are *absolutely* possible in my life.

> *"I can do all things through Christ who strengthens me."*—Philippians 4:13

Book cover illustrated by Tiffany McBride
Review on back of book by Karen Robinson
Book edited by Joseph Ferry
Book edited by D'Vorah Bailey
Book formatted by Maggie McLaughlin
Book Launched on Amazon by Maggie McLaughlin
Mock-up book design for marketing by Kimberly Malone
Book cover formatted by Kimberly Malone

www.ingramcontent.com/pod-product-compliance
Lightning Source LLC
Chambersburg PA
CBHW071140130626
46553CB00004B/1460